# Real Estate Marketing How to Be a Real-Estate Millionaire

By

**Ernie Braveboy**

# Introduction

I want to thank you and congratulate you for downloading the book, *"Real Estate Marketing How to Be a Real-Estate Millionaire"*.

This book has actionable information on how to become a real estate millionaire by marketing real estate like a pro.

Real estate is undoubtedly one of the most stable investment vehicles world over. This explains why almost every billionaire has interests in real estate. Luckily, with real estate, you don't have to be a billionaire or millionaire to get started; you can make money with real estate without owning any property!

How is that so? Well, you can do that by being a real estate agent, marketer, flipping houses, wholesaling and much, much more. The good news is that you can make thousands of dollars per deal, which puts you on a very unique position to make millions of dollars a year.

And if you are looking for comprehensive information on how to make a million dollars as a real estate agent, this book has all you need to follow to get there. In this book, you will discover what it takes to be a real estate marketer, the different ways in which you can make money and how you can actually make money from being a real estate marketer. Whether you are a real estate agent, wholesaler, flipper or homeowner looking to sell your property, you will find this book very helpful in ensuring you close a deal fast. Let's begin.

Thanks again for downloading this book. I hope you enjoy it!

# Table of Contents

# Real Estate Marketing: A Background

Marketing is at the core of real estate; it is the fuel that drives real estate. Think about it; whether you are an agent, developer, a wholesaler, a flipper or a homeowner wishing to sell, rent out or lease out your property, you MUST unleash the full power of marketing to generate leads and ultimately attract customers who are willing and able to pay the selling price or the rent amount. However, the purpose of this book is not just about selling property one off; it is about making a business out of it so that you can sell to all types of customers repeatedly.

The thing with real estate marketing is that it has to be continual; you don't just do it once then sit back to get people desperately looking for your property to rent/buy. It is just like any other worthwhile course like losing weight; you really don't expect that exercising once and eating the right foods once will make you lose 10 pounds instantly irrespective of how extreme your measures are. You have to commit to eating right and exercising if you are keen on making any significant progress over time. Similarly, with real estate, you must market effectively and consistently to see any real progress.

The question is; how can you do it effectively to a point of being able to make millions of dollars from your craft?

Well, that's what we will get straight into starting with the first step i.e. finding property that you will be marketing because when you think about it, if you have no property to market, you have no business being a real estate marketer.

**Note:** Keep in mind that I already stated that with real estate marketing, you don't have to own the property that you are marketing. Let's begin there.

## Step 1: Find Property to Sell: How to Find the Best Sellers

There are many ways to find sellers of real estate, and anyone will tell you to check the newspaper ads, buy leads from websites, put up signs inscribed 'we are buying houses', sending advertisements and so on. I'm sure you know about these strategies and even more.

Most of these strategies are okay and will get you real estate property. However, my strategy is different. I don't just look for sellers; I look for the best sellers and the best sellers according to me are:

1. People who are willing to sell their property for a low price, a very low price; this generally means selling it somewhere between 10% - 30% of market value. Sounds impossible I know, but it's not.

2. Again, the best sellers are people willing to sell their property with flexible terms. This means that I'm targeting a seller who will accept to finance the property for you, require no cash down and also charge no interest (0% interest).

As you will soon note, our aim is coming up with a list of the prospective sellers and mailing them immediately, this is how you do it:

Begin by finding a targeted list of various property owners who are extremely motivated to actually sell. Ideally, you aren't looking for just every list of property owners; you are looking for very specific property owners who are more likely to sell their property than the usual owner. We have a number of ways to go about acquiring these lists and obviously, some methods can work better than others depending on your area.

## The first option: Work with the county

In this case, you'll be looking for your county's delinquent tax list. This is a list you will not lack in every county and this list always contains a goldmine of info that can assist you to pin down some of the most motivated sellers in your locality.

NOTE: A city, township or county keeps a detailed record of every property within its area of jurisdiction to be able to charge taxes effectively. This means that they have information on the following:

- The property's owner

- How much is paid for the property

- How much the owner owes in taxes

Among other details

All this info is in the public records and thus, you can find this data on any property you want in the US. Most county websites will provide this information for free even though sometimes their systems tend to be confusing to work with. Luckily, we have other services such as; agentpro 247 (discussed in the next point) that will provide about the same data, only in a package that's easier to understand. For example:

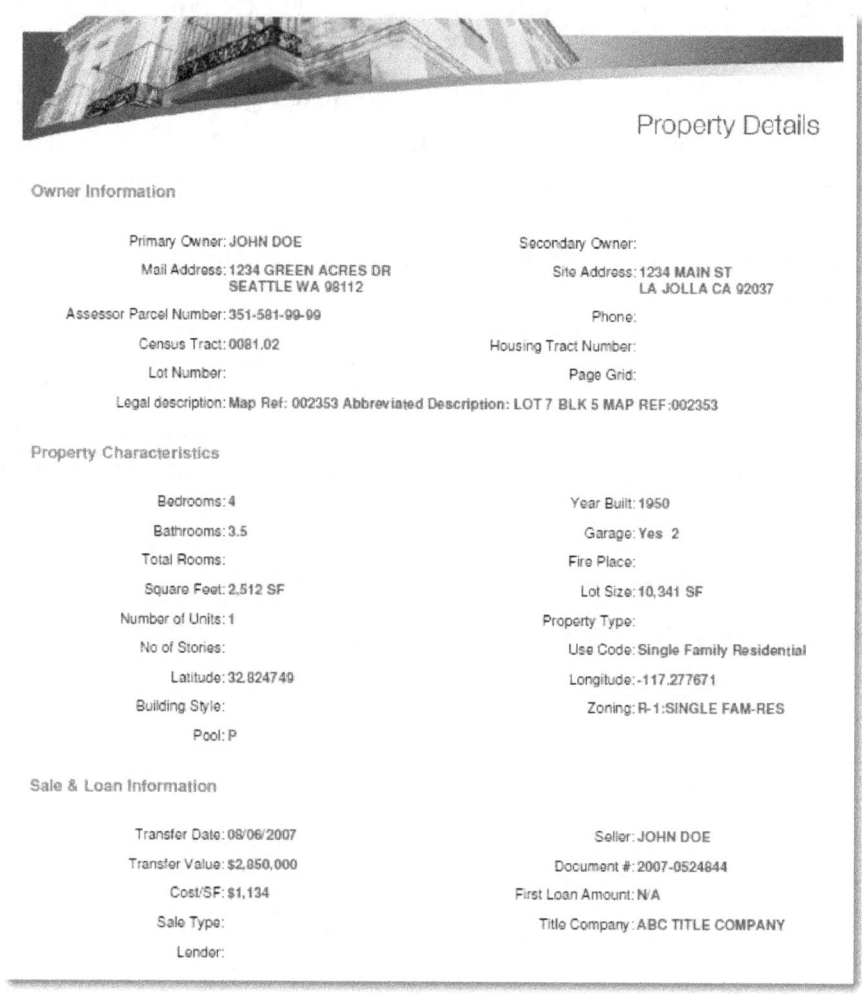

(You can thus use the service when you find difficulty employing this method.)

Therefore, when property owners fail to pay their taxes, the county treasurer creates a running list of such people-which is basically the same list the county uses to mail out the delinquent tax notices.

You have to note that there are many people in this list who will be very willing to sell their property at a very steep discount- and most of them rarely want to advertise their desperation. They need somebody like you to 'help' them and make the whole process idiot-proof.

It is not always easy to get this information though- you have to expect the list to cost you something. Most county treasurers might charge you something to give you the list.

The good thing about this method is that you always get fresh and accurate data because anyway, it is coming from the database in real time.

### The second option: Working with a data provider

You can also get this list from a data service dealing with real estate.

We have numerous data companies that can give you these lists in a clean and workable format. While some are expensive, some are reasonably cheap and if you understand what type of property you are looking for, your search might end here.

These data companies comb through almost all the counties in the United States and make it very easy to find property.

Let's take one example:

### AgentPro247

AgentPro247 is a service that offers public record information. This means that you can actually look up any property in a few minutes and find the info you need.

This service is one of the easiest to use, to sign up and offers one of the best property research tools you can ever find. Unlike the counties, it is not just about the lists but also about the ease of the due diligence process, especially for niche property types like vacant land.

One thing I appreciate about this service is that their system informs you just how current their database is in each county in the country.

Other data providers providing that could assist you in a similar way to get this list include the following:

- ReboGateway

- RealQuest

- Melissa Data

- ListSource

You job now is to use the data provider to target or sort lists based on these characteristics:

- Out-of-state property owners (those living outside the county): People living out-of-state are usually more disconnected and disengaged from their properties. For whatever reason, many of them had to move away unexpectedly and chances are they have a vested interest in liquidating as soon as they can.

Other characteristics you might want to consider include:

- Absentee owners or people who aren't living in their property

- Property owners who've owed their property for ten or more years

- Property owners with delinquent taxes

- Properties in good price range

*Send the message*

Once you pull your list and sort it out, the next step is sending the mail to the owner. The process of doing so can be simple or difficult, depending on the method- for instance, if you've ever tried putting together a bulk mail campaign on your own before, you must know how dreary it can be. This is why we have to use Click2Mail.

Click2Mail is a service that can allow you upload your pre-sorted list, your postcard template and send your bulk email campaigns without any production work needed. It will print, stamp and mail everything for you and charge postage rates and production costs, which are typically lower than you would otherwise incur if you choose to stamp and mail the postcards in-house. The process is amazingly simple- check out the picture below to learn more.

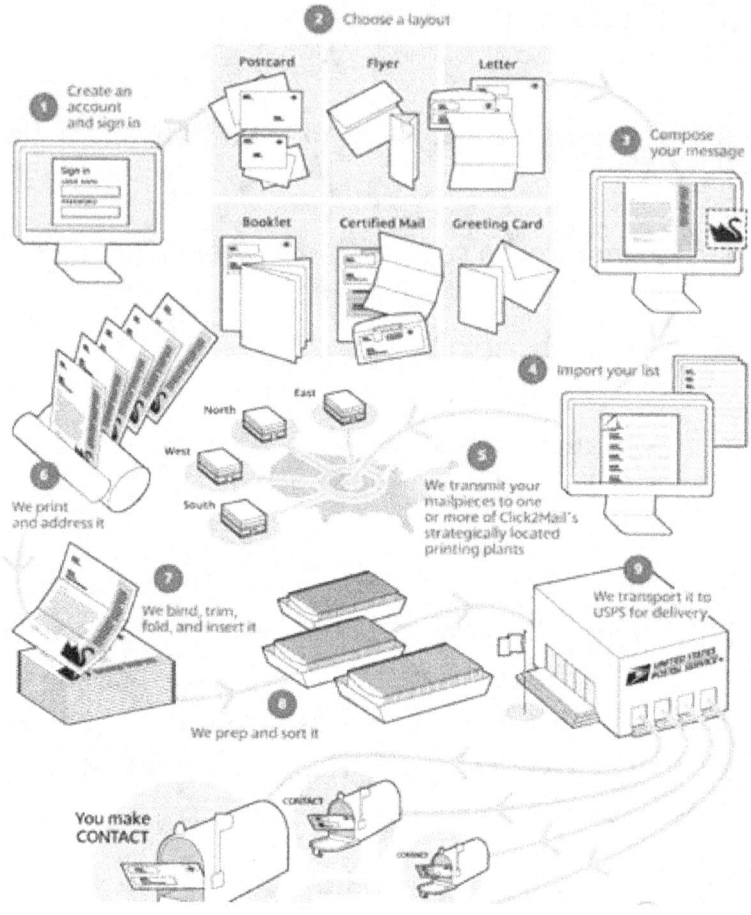

When you contact the recipient and settle on a good deal, it is time to market the property:

- Get to know more about the property so that you are able to sell what you understand in and out.

- Take good pictures and create high quality videos of the property to post on your website to market it as from this point, our focus is on the buyer.

***Side note:***

Before you start marketing the property though, you have to understand your investment strategy; what kind of a marketer are you? While you will find business people purchasing property and selling it using the 'buy and hold' or flipping techniques, most marketers don't technically own any property; most marketers are largely wholesalers or just plain agents.

*Who is a wholesaler?*

A wholesaler is a person who looks for good deals in real estate, writes a contract to acquire the deal and then sells that contract to another buyer. This means that the wholesaler doesn't actually own the property he/she is selling but puts a property, say a distressed home, under contract so that he/she assigns that contract to another buyer. The wholesaler then markets the home to prospective buyers for a price higher than they placed the property under contract for. You can therefore view a wholesaler as a person or a middleman who gets money for finding deals. As a wholesaler, you can sell your contract to retail buyers or just sell them to investors (like house flippers) referred to as the 'cash buyers'. When you're dealing with these cash buyers, you get money within weeks or even days and can easily create robust connections in the real estate network. You can read more about wholesaling at https://fitsmallbusiness.com/how-to-wholesale-real-estate/ for more information.

As I stated earlier, you can also choose to become a flipper- a strategy that is not common to folks who've decided to focus on real estate marketing. A flipper purchases real estate property at a discounted price, develops or improves it over time and then sells it for profit. This is similar to the other strategy referred to as 'buy and hold' where the investor buys property and holds it so that he sells it in future for a better price. Between the time of buying and selling, he/she could rent it out to get extra money.

If at all you want to take on any of these investment strategies (apart from being a plain agent/marketer), you might find the first one (wholesaling) more appealing than the rest if you want to mainly focus on being a marketer.

**Note:**

Ideally, you need to ensure that you make a profit depending on what you do. If you are into flipping, then you have to consider such things like expected cost of repair, your expected profit and the value of property after repair. Using these three will help you to determine the price you should pay for any property on sale to ensure you don't end up burning yourself accidentally. You can use https://investfourmore.com/fix-and-flip-70-percent-rule-calculator/ or http://www.pinefinancialgroup.com/fix-and-flip-calculator-iphone-app/. You can as well use http://www.creditfinanceplus.com/calculators/house-flipping-net-profit.php. You can learn how to determine the value of property after repair using the guidelines https://www.creonline.com/how-to-determine-market-value.html As for determining the expected cost of repair, you can refer to https://www.auction.com/blog/how-to-properly-estimate-repair-costs-on-a-flip/, https://investfourmore.com/2014/11/03/much-cost-fix-repair-house/ and https://patchofland.com/blog/all-projects/2017/04/11/how-to-estimate-repair-costs-accurately-when-flipping-a-property/. Issues to do with the nitty gritties of flipping and wholesaling are really outside the scope of this book. However, the guidelines above will make it very easy for you to follow the whole process with a lot of ease until you find the right property to market.

The truth is; you shouldn't have a hard time finding property to market if you follow the guidelines above. Now that you have property to market, it is time to come up with a clear plan/strategy because as you are well aware, failing to plan/strategize is synonymous with planning/strategizing to fail. That's why the next thing we will be discussing is strategy.

# Step 2: Develop Your Real Estate Marketing Strategy

As a real estate marketer, you can go online, stick to the offline methods or use both of them. If you want to incorporate the online tactics, you need to first of all think about real estate marketing that incorporates web design, online lead generation and search marketing among others. Your digital strategy is important all the way through-regardless of the stage of the process you are in (whether pre-development or post-development). Therefore, my assumption is that you already have a website.

## Do you have a real estate marketing website?

If you don't, the first thing you should probably do is get a good, topnotch website. You have two options: create one yourself if you have some bit of knowledge of how to go about it or hire a professional to do it for you. You can hire a professional from Fiverr.com, Upwork.com, Guru.com, Freelancer.com or Peopleperhour.com. If you are an intermediate computer user, you can use a website builder like those shown at
http://www.top10bestwebsitebuilders.com/comparison

Why is this important?

### A few tips...

Potential clients want to work with a person they can trust, a person who's looking out for them and can offer valuable advice along the way. Your website is now your first meet and greet.

The website's content is everything; from headlines to navigation, videos, images, blogs- all the components that tell the story of your brand.

When a visitor lands on your site, they naturally base the quality of your listings and services off what they see; and even though we are often taught not to judge a book by its cover when growing up, in this situation, the cover is everything. Consider that the largest part of this market is visual, so you have to use large, bold and beautiful images. You need to allow your properties to speak for themselves.

Again, we have more and more websites incorporating flat designs and doing away with three dimension elements - they pay attention to flat colors and typography (the styles, colors and fonts that identify your brand). This design gives your site a fresh, modern appearance.

Perhaps you need to also know that today, sites are really growing off responsive background videos and images. You have only a couple of seconds to catch the attention of the user, so showcase your most attractive and desirable properties with beautiful and high resolution visuals.

I really don't consider having a website in this day and age part of a plan; it is a must have so as you start planning, you MUST have the essentials first.

The first strategy is planning. Without it, everything else would be largely unworkable.

NOTE: The steps of the plan as discussed below are only an overview of what you'll do from here. We'll discuss in more detail some important parts of it in the subsequent parts of this book. So don't worry when it all seems too much or complicated to gather.

### Create a Marketing Plan

Before the plan can commence, you have to set realistic and specific goals. You need to decide what you really want your real estate marketing endeavors to fulfill as this will help you to set clear expectations for all your social media presence, website, email campaigns, blog, among other tactics to take on.

With the four steps provided below, you will be able to fully plan your real estate marketing strategy.

### Outline the 4Ws of real estate marketing

The 4Ws refer to "Who, What, Where and When" which is a good place to start in creating your plan. You can be general at first with the 'Ws' but over time, you can make them more specific. For example, if the idea you have about your general audience is broad (perhaps all sellers in a single community instead of sellers in a specific price bracket), that's okay. You can come back to these Ws and then tweak them accordingly. To get started though, write them down so that you have some understanding of how you'll structure your real estate marketing plan.

From this point onwards, the book will be based on a plan that contains the following milestones and objectives below.

*The who: determine your target audience*

*The when: determine a timetable for success*

*The where: identify the platforms to take with your marketing*

*The what: implement your plan and identify the metrics you'll build upon*

## 1: Determine Your Target Audience

Knowing who to market to is important; and forms a big part of the battle. Make sure to target a suitable niche group of purchasers and sellers with whom you have worked in the past or who you'd want to market to. Also, do not worry if you cannot yet isolate an exact demographic you think is best to reach as narrowing your focus even a bit will improve your success greatly.

There's one factor that you need to consider though when selecting a primary audience: think of your past client- if you've had any. If you have not earned much money off a particular segment of sellers and buyers, perhaps you should think about marketing to a new group; but if you're contented with your revenue in the recent months and years, you can keep to marketing to the same audience.

Another factor to consider is the housing market statistics: what do they indicate? Currently, the figures that relate to income, home sales, property values and many other areas greatly have a profound influence on the marketing decisions for brokers and agents throughout the nation. You need to look for this data for your local market to decide the kind of people who are worth pursuing and who are not. For instance, if the statistics indicate that in your community, millennials are purchasing the majority of homes for sale, chances are they would make a good core audience.

## 2: Determine a Timetable for Success

As you will note, there is not really an exact length of time it takes a professional and brand to see significant results from their marketing efforts. Nonetheless, this does not mean you cannot have specific goals to aim for in the long haul. Take a look at these examples of goals to aspire to after different periods.

- After a month- since your marketing is just getting started or going, you could aim to increase more awareness of your company online. When you gain acknowledgement as a successful real estate firm in your area, it means you are doing very well so far.

- After 3 months- about a quarter into your plan, you could target moderate goals related to social media followers, lead gen, site traffic , general online inquiries from clients and potential new contacts

- After 6 months- after the first year into your strategy, you should have greater ambitions such as getting a particular amount of targeted seller leads or a particular number of closed deals.

It wouldn't do you much good to look out further than a year down the line because it's very difficult to expect what will change over the course of 12 months with your business. You should thus set goals for the future that can be easily foreseen.

## 3: Identify the Platforms/Avenues/Tactics to Take With Your Marketing

After knowing your marketing demographic, choose the methods or channels you want to use in order to support your business. Definitely, the core group of tactics such as email, social media blogging and using a website are all the ones you should use from the beginning, but you shouldn't be afraid of trying other useful marketing ploys such as hosting podcasts or webinars, creating infographics and creating long-form content such as reports, e-books and so forth.

You will never know which tactics work best with you unless you try a variety of them. Also don't forget that your website is the foundation of all your marketing activities since your audience is led there by most of your marketing activities- if not all.

We'll go through some of the best marketing methods or avenues you can use but before that, we have to consider something first:

### The marketing costs

Before taking up any marketing strategy or tasks, you need to consider the costs involved compared to how much you are willing to spend.

While most marketing tasks require your time, some require a good amount of financial investment as well. You can create blog posts and other written content without spending anything significant- just find stats, news and other information to curate from other publications or simply create 'how-to' articles of your own based on your know-how and experiences- just like that, you have information to share with your audience.

On the other hand, we have the paid campaigns- which is mainly advertising. These require a more detailed plan and money. For the paid advertising efforts, you can take a closer look at your revenue for the past couple of months as well as the much you are expecting to earn in the subsequent months. After that, you can apportion part of this amount for your ad spend. You could use the following paid advertising avenues:

Google AdWords- here, you can efficiently reach a qualified audience by targeting certain keywords.

Facebook AdWords- you'll be offered display ads that can be featured in News Feeds and sides of pages. Advertisements on such a platform provide a unique way to reach your audience in a targeted manner- that is to say, designating exactly who views your advertisement according to demographic criteria such as location, interests and age.

Twitter ads- you can promote your whole twitter account or certain tweets in the same way as Facebook ads. Every so often, Twitter adds new ad options for brands- so you need to research the page- 'Twitter for business' to view the opportunities that could work for you.

Google Display Network ads- while you can create advertisements to appear in the search results for different terms related to your local market and business, you can also aim for certain sites on which to have the ads displayed.

The above examples are part of the online strategies. Offline strategies like using billboards or holding seminars can also cost you more than others like using bandit signs.

NOTE: Whatever the types of ads you choose, you need to do more research on the merits and demerits of each. Either way, you should investigate each ad option- One or more of them could assist you reach buyers and sellers better.

Let's now see examples of tactics you could use to drive people to your website, to give you an idea of where to start if you became absolutely clueless.

# Step 3: Taking Action

# Online Strategies

### 1: Email Marketing

Email marketing is still very effective in our digital world of instant messages, tweets and quick moving news feeds. Therefore, it always works to send interesting, informational and newsworthy newsletters to your sphere of influence because:

People are always checking their email throughout the day and you thus have the opportunity to get yourself into their inbox. The good thing with real estate marketing is that most people will look at houses, as it is very difficult to resist clicking a picture of a beautiful kitchen!

As a rule of thumb, you need to note that many people find their dream home when they aren't looking and thus, a targeted email newsletter is a good way to catch their interest.

So, get started, sign up with an email marketing service such as Mailchimp. You will note that many such companies actually offer a free service, which includes tips and templates on creating and sending a perfect newsletter. You will also be able to monitor your results by seeing the open rate and also the number of people who clicked on links to your listings. You can use these results to inform sellers that their home has been viewed.

Other popular email marketing services include:

AWeber- Its platform is easy to get started with and it also connects to other platforms like WordPress seamlessly. What's more, you are able to access ready to use email templates, autoresponders, email tracking and autoresponders with it.

ConvertKit- this is a strong platform that is commonly used by marketers, authors as well as professional bloggers. It allows you to (among other things) offer content upgrades and incentives together with email signup forms. It also comes with auto-responders that are easy to manage which lets you send drip emails.

GetResponse- highly regarded as one of the top email marketing solutions, GetResponse is easy to use and makes email marketing for fresh startups seem so simple. It has great marketing automation tools that allow you to create smart automated campaigns. You can create campaigns, send content designed for specific groups and segment contacts with a drag and drop builder. These tools are sure to help you create effective campaigns to boost your profits.

*Tip:*

1. Emails are a great way to get your brand and expertise out there. They can and actually should have up-to-date-listings, but also let folks know you are on top of your game with everything that's going on in the market within your location.

2. Moreover, people are always researching online for homes but when they are selecting an agent, they want a personal connection. If you want to be identified as an expert in your area, you have to ensure you include local

items in your email; list of remarkable hardware stores and nurseries, a detailed review of restaurants, a recommendation for a resident contractor and so on.

Please learn more about how to setup your email marketing program at https://www.campaignmonitor.com/resources/guides/getting-started-with-email-marketing/.

## 2: *Social Media Engagement*

The different social media platforms are a fantastic way to promote and sell your listings, engage with your followers, grow your network, promote and sell your listings and attract buyers as well as sellers too. Let's take one example:

### Facebook

You need to start with your inner circle to build up your network- and Facebook is a great avenue to do that. From my own experience, the people who know about you will easily get excited quickly about your real estate trade as it is a great platform to let people know who you are and there's something fresh and awesome you are doing that should be taken seriously, and also grow your circle of influence at the same time.

Post your videos on your pages, groups, timelines and even inbox your friends directly with the videos and pictures.

Update your occupation, post real estate tips, start real conversations with people about what you've learned and perhaps also where you hope your career will go. It is possible you will like the results even if you only invest a couple of minutes per day.

Other popular platforms include

- LinkedIn

- Tweeter

- Instagram

- Snapchat

- Pinterest

**Note**: As a real estate agent, you cannot afford not to have a Facebook page because it can help you generate leads for your website and engage prospects with greater ease. And if you could combine it with YouTube and other social medial platforms that use images like Pinterest and Instagram, you will find generate leads with greater ease.

Generally, posting and tweeting your listings gets them viewed by many people and you can include information that might not be shared by a regular newspaper or postcard ad.

The most important thing you have to remember when using social media to market real estate is that it works best when you view and handle it as a two way street. It is imperative you comment, like and share posts of other members (not just focusing on publishing your own). The more engagement your post receives, the more views it receives. Acknowledging other people's comments on your post is also another way to show that you are well engaged in your social media presence which will not only help get your post become viewed by more people, but assist you start a conversation and attract more followers.

### 3: Paid Advertising/Campaigns

We'll first look at Facebook ads in detail before taking a brief look at Google AdWords.

### How to set up Facebook ads

Note: you need to make sure your website is formatted properly so that you don't risk reducing the number of people opting in to your message significantly.

In this regard, there are some things you can do to make your website convert properly.

*Not familiar with the term* **conversion** *(in websites)?*

*Conversion refers to getting your visitors or users to perform what you want-whether it's buying your product, signing up for your newsletter, downloading a whitepaper, registering for a webinar or even filling a lead or contact form. Website conversion is thus most critical factor to the success of online marketing strategy. This is because if your website is to generate any qualified leads, the visitor should be able to open the channels of communication by either subscribing, sharing, saving etc.*

*Conversion rate on the other hand refers to the percentage of users who take a particular desired action. For instance:*

*Let's assume your website is visited by 100,000 users during the month of December. And 2000 users purchased or requested to see your property from the site. Thus, the conversion rate of your website is 2% (2,000/100,000)*

- Write blogs that are simple to read (at least one for every business day).

In this case, even the titles matter, and since simple word changes can tremendously increase or reduce conversions, companies like Buzzffeed and Groupon spend millions of dollars split testing headlines. You can gain from this for free. Simply go to <u>buzzsumo.com</u> and enter 'real estate'. You will find the most popular articles on real estate on the web- just pick ten titles and begin writing considering that all these titles are all pre-tested. Actually, everything about writing a post has all been laid out for you.

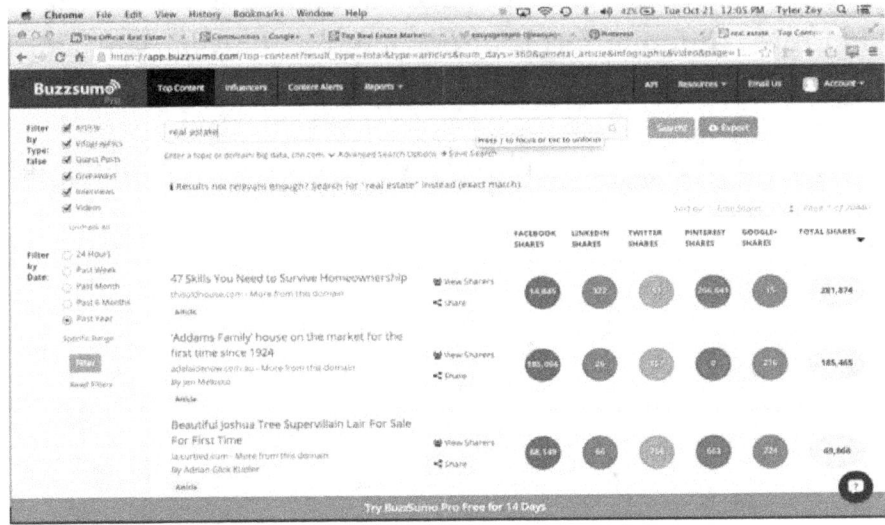

- Each blog requires a graphic to go with it. This makes sure your Facebook ads for real estate convert well.

You can order some graphics from a site like Fiverr.com for as little as $5. Just ensure to look for someone offering 'flat design', as this is a trend that came out not so long ago that gives graphics a very sharp appearance.

NOTE: Good graphics tend to drive people to convert into your email list and actually share their contact.

*Conversion techniques*

You need ways to drive people to convert onto your email list on your website. I would recommend that you have four different kinds of email capture boxes. Just ensure every one of them is offering something different in exchange for the email address and phone number.

Take the following example:

You can have one landing page containing a capture form and three different forms of opt-in boxes on your site, all of which are making different offers.

A good example of an opt-in box (if you're not familiar with this term):

## WHAT IF YOUR COPY DIDN'T BORE THE CRAP OUTTA PROSPECTS?

**You've only got so much time to write emails and landing pages. Stop wasting your time - and your visitors' time - on weak attempts.**

Your best email addy

Teach Me How, Joanna!

✓ Get a free 120-page persuasion guide
✓ Get a free 7-part copy mini-course
✓ Be the first to hear about cool shizzle

After that, input the headline you chose from Buzzsumo as the headline on the opt-in box or landing page. When someone subscribes to your email list, make sure you send them the free content.

Well, Congratulations! Your site now has great content that people want to read.

My assumption is that at this point, your site is well set up to receive a good number of phone numbers and email addresses from any traffic sent to it. You can prime the site with paid traffic and we're going to do that using Facebook ads so that we get the phone contacts and email addresses.

We are going to start with Facebook ads, which I'll explain how to set up step by step then move on to Google AdWords, which are usually more costly and competitive.

- Choose 3 of your favorite articles you did about your business and head over to the Facebook <u>website</u>.

- Click the button labeled 'manage your ads'.

- Next, go ahead and click 'create ads'.

- After that, choose 'clicks to website'.

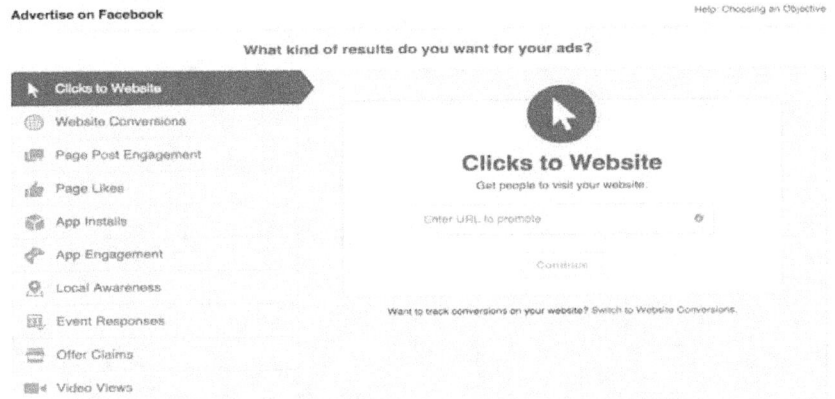

- Now enter the URL to the best article you've written on your site.

- The image you designed should appear below. You will want to choose three other images from the stock image library of Facebook. This will assist you split test your ads.

- After that, connect your Facebook page.

- Input the title of your article in the little 'headline' box then write a short description.

- Now turn on the Mobile Newsfeed Ads ad Newsfeed Ads.

- Turn off the Partner Mobile Aps and Sidebar ads because they don't really convert as well when you're running Facebook Ads especially for Real Estate.

Congratulations for completing that part. Let's now discuss how to set up ads for real estate.

I recommend the following demographics:

| | |
|---|---|
| Locations | United States, Missouri |
| | Kansas City + 25 mi |
| | Add a country, state/province, city or ZIP |
| Age | 25 ▾ - 55 ▾ |
| Gender | **All** Men Women |
| Languages | Enter a language... |
| Relationship Status | **In a relationship** ✕ |
| | **Married** ✕ |
| | **Engaged** ✕ |
| | Choose relationship statuses     Browse |
| Education Level | **College grad** ✕ |
| | **Associate degree** ✕ |
| | Choose education statuses     Browse |
| Income | **Income ($50,000 - $75,000)** ✕ |
| | **Income ($75,000 - $100,000)** ✕ |
| | **Income ($100,000 - $125,000)** ✕ |
| | **Income (over $125,000)** ✕ |
| | Choose income     Browse |
| | More Demographics ▾ |
| Interests | Search interests    Suggestions   Browse |
| Behaviors | Residential profiles |
| | Likely to move |
| | Search behaviors     Browse |

At this point, we have the ads set up. You'll want to set up the budget at something about $200- $500 per month. I would recommend you begin with $350 per month. The Facebook advertisements for real estate do create a scalable source leads for you. You can choose to turn them up or down and spend however much you want to on them.

You should also click the part labeled 'optimize for clicks' and 'manually set your Bid per click'. Fix the bid $.10 over the maximum recommended amount.

Now head back and repeat the entire process for two of your articles.

You now have your Facebook Ads to show your message to prospective homebuyers within the area. They will be directed to your website where you'll get their phone number, email address and name.

*What to do each day when running the Facebook ads*

Since your ad is set up; the next thing you have to do is monitor it only once per day. While you're monitoring them, ensure you adjust your cost per click up or down based on the recommendation of Facebook and how much impression you're able to see. If your ad is not being shown to anyone, it means you are too low with your bid- you will easily detect this when your number of impressions stop changing every day.

Second, you can monitor the images you use on your Facebook ads. These images have a great impact on conversion. Some of them will convert better than others. You can use those images and delete the rest.

Turn off the ads that seem to cost more per click than the rest and then go over to the ad that is cheapest and click 'create similar ad'. Change the image into something similar to that ad (but that which is still different).

This will assist you in finding the best converting ad. It might take you a month to find the best one.

Lastly, you can set up three headlines and monitor the one that converts the best and consider shutting one of them off.

To validate this ad spend, let's do some math:

*The math for Real Estate Facebook Ads*

Usually, 10 percent of the Facebook ads clicks will give you their email address or phone number or both. You should always aim to produce better articles and content in general on your site until you get higher than the 10 percent conversion rate.

I'm sure you have a number at the back of your mind that turn into finished transactions. You can use the formula below to justify the ad cots:

Monthly Ad Spend / Cost Per Click = Total Clicks To Website

Clicks * Conversion Rate = Total Number Of Leads

Leads * Your Close Rate = Total Houses Sold

Alternatively:

$350 (total amount you spend in a month) / $0.35 (the average cost per click = 1000 clicks to your website

The 1000 clicks * the 10% conversion rate = 100 contacts

100 leads * Y% (your conversion rate) = Y properties sold

These are simple equations that should assist you validate the $350 ad spend. Once you find a profitable funnel, you can now open up the budget and gage it.

## Google AdWords

Google AdWords is the system developed by Google to help you market your services and products in Google Search Engine, including its affiliate sites through the use of a placed text advertisement which pops up when people are searching for phrases related to what you're offering- which appears as a 'sponsored link'. The system is basically a pay-per-click system, which means you can direct where your advertisement should appear via bidding for a sequence of phrases. You also pay the amount you have bid for only if somebody clicks on your ad.

The ad appears on the results page you want to appear in; for example, the first page of Google for a search result. Your ads will appear to the right side and top of the organic search results. Through the amount of money you bid, you can also pitch at the spot on the page you want your ad to appear. This may crudely mean the more you bid for a phrase, the higher your ad appears on the first page of the search results.

You have to note that most people rarely scan past the first page of the search results, and also that the higher your website is located on a page, the more visitors your website gets because web users generally prefer clicking on the search results or ads at the top of the page.

To set up Google AdWords, just follow steps at https://www.entrepreneur.com/article/237212.

### Video Marketing: Use the Viral Video Strategy

Viral videos are not just sloppy or amateur videos of dogs doing funny things or celebrities doing weird things. In fact, some of the best viral videos have been produced professionally by companies to be able to reach their audience differently.

When it comes to real estate, a viral video is one that promotes a property creatively, including a real estate company or an agent (or both) by use of content that draws attention and inspires viewers to want to share it with other people.

### *What makes a video go viral?*

Viral videos in what can often be a pretty conservative industry ought to have one or most of a number of the characteristics to be able to achieve the success of an average viral video, which include:

*Funny*-The easiest way to get your video to go viral quickly is by making it funny. Nonetheless, there is a catch: working out what funny is to your target audience. There is nothing as bad as a video that is trying to be funny but is either way off the mark or tasteless. Therefore, make sure you know your audience pretty well before creating any video you wish to go viral.

*Creative*- You know your video is creative when another person watches it and says 'ah, wish I'd thought of that.' Creativity is respected in all social circles and can do a great job at attracting the interest of viewers.

*Short*- If you go over some of the best viral videos on YouTube, you'll realize that most of them are actually less than five minutes long. The viral videos spread very quickly largely because most of them are extremely easy to absorb and watch many times.

*Memorable-* You'll know your video has gone viral when folks begin referring to it by name and if people can remember your video, they are most probably going to contact you when they want to do business.

The process of making a video is quite simple and straightforward:

### How to make a real estate marketing video

Log in to https://app.picovico.com/login

Gather the pictures and video clips you want to use. Assuming you want to make a video about a particular real estate property (a bungalow, maybe). All you require is taking as many attractive photos and video clips as possible and filtering the best ones to include in the video.

Select the style you want to use. You have to choose a style at the beginning of your video making process. For the real estate videos, I might suggest you go for styles such as Frameless and circle but you can use any other style you think would be suitable for the video.

Upload the media files. You can now upload all your clips and photos you want to use onto the workspace in the site. For the music, I would suggest you use the free or commercially useable music since you will be using the video for purposes of branding or advertising.

Preview and complete. Take a preview of the video to see how it will look like and then you decide whether to go back to editing or just finalize the video. After that, you'll be allowed to add a title to your video followed by a description.

Save and share. Once the video is complete, you can download it and upload it to any platform you want such as YouTube, Vimeo or even the Picovico video page.

https://youtu.be/IF6anKHo1lU a good example of what I'm talking about.

## Write regular newsletters

Real estate newsletters can be an effective marketing tool for keeping your name top of mind with your current clients, past clients, your prospects as well as your sphere of influence. They deliver your message, reinforce your brand and demonstrate your expertise- which is what a successful marketer does regularly.

## The steps of creating newsletters

I am going to use MailChimp to describe this process. MailChimp is one of the best services for email marketing campaigns today especially because it has great free packages.

### Gather your news

You have to spend quite some time gathering great content if you are to have a great newsletter. If you are sending a monthly newsletter, save some articles you find during the month in a special folder so that you have the entire content in a single area. You can get your content from anywhere-for instance, when you meet your friends, workmates (during staff meetings), let them know that you are looking for articles and request them to share their wisdom.

You can also go through the internet to get great content ideas, which could be about the following:

- The current market statistics- this means numbering the homes that are listed for sales, giving the medium or average listing and the sale price, and also the average days on the market. Make sure to interpret the data you present, explain well what it means and show how it is trending over time.

- The properties sold recently- sellers and buyers love seeing what has sold recently. Make sure you follow your brokers and the rules and regulations in your local state on what and how to present the current sales.

- The upcoming activities- It is recommended that you have a list or calendar of forthcoming events and or activities in a given area. This is important because most real estate newsletters tend to be very much targeted for a given geographical location. It sort of helps keep the newsletter 'sticky' and gives folks a reason to keep your newsletter and refer back to it multiple times.

- A CTA (call to action) - Getting your name and message out is important and a newsletter should also contain a CTA to inspire engagement. You can give a free home valuation/CMA. Insert a link to a webpage that is specifically created for that particular newsletter to enable recipients to go and download any information that they might be looking for. Try doing a CTA that informs people how you can set them up for automatic updates for listing.

- The seasonal tips- you can also include a short article and perhaps links to articles on issues related to taxes. You need to keep it specific to real estate and if possible, add some info about mortgage deduction.

  Is the school about to resume? Include back to school tips where people can find school supplies.

Other things you can include are:

- More financial news- such as rate cuts, home loans, first home owner grants and new laws.

- Home improvement news and tips

- Time specific news- such as home security tips and news during the holidays

- Process news – such as the selling and purchasing processes of homes

*Edit the news*

After gathering your content, scan your article for simple things like sentence construction and grammar mistakes. In any case, the best articles are typically ones that are short and sharp. Make sure the article heading matches the content and take out any industry jargon or waffle.

NOTE: If you've never worked with MailChimp before, you can read http://mailchimp.com/resources/guides/getting-started-with-mailchimp/ to get started in case you find yourself getting lost anywhere.

*Create your list*

This is basically the list of the email addresses of people you want to receive your newsletter. When you create an account and sign in to MailChimp, you can start by creating your mail out list.

**4. Create your campaign.** Click on good ol' regular campaign if this is the first time you are doing this.

Regular Ol' Campaign

Send a lovely HTML email along with a plain-text alternative version

Plain-Text Campaign

Send a simple plain-text email with no pictures or formatting

A/B Split Campaign

Send to two groups to determine the best subject line, from name, or time/day to send campaigns
learn more

RSS-Driven Campaign

Send content from an RSS feed to a list
learn more

Email Beamer: Send From Your Email Client

Did you know you can send campaigns directly from your favorite email client? learn more

After creating the list, pick this list and begin entering the details about your campaign- or the newsletter.

*The templates*

Depending on how you want your newsletter to appear, you can pick any options from the ones below:

If you want to have full control over the layout and are good with code, you can write (code) your own.

If you still want to have control and are not confident that you have enough coding skills to take up the challenge, then perhaps the 'drag and drop' option is ideal for you.

However, if you want an option that has no fuss, you can select the pre-designed option. Let me demonstrate the predesigned option for you.

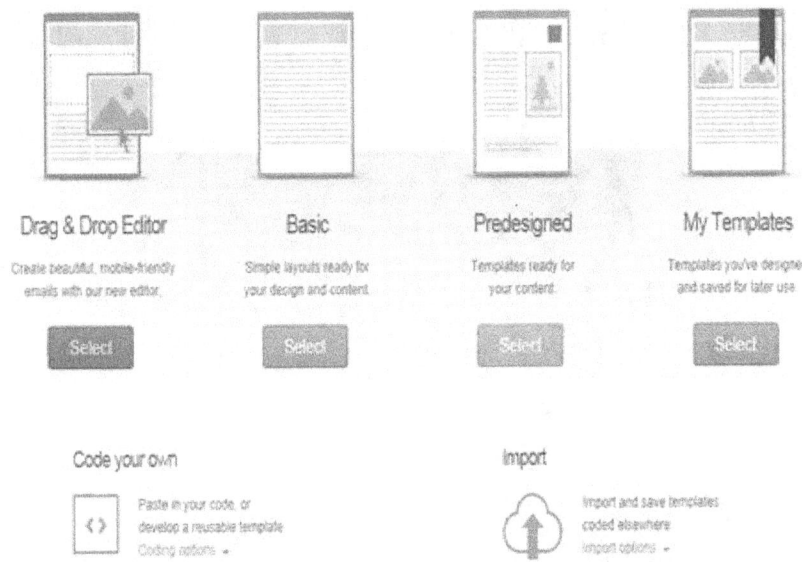

## Select a Template Option

**Drag & Drop Editor**
Create beautiful, mobile-friendly emails with our new editor.
Select

**Basic**
Simple layouts ready for your design and content.
Select

**Predesigned**
Templates ready for your content.
Select

**My Templates**
Templates you've designed and saved for later use
Select

**Code your own**
Paste in your code, or develop a reusable template
Coding options

**Import**
Import and save templates coded elsewhere
Import options

The good thing with MailChimp and services like it is that everything is done for you and anyone who has limited or exposure to the online newsletters will find it very simple. Just click on the templates on the column to the left and select a design that best fits your business.

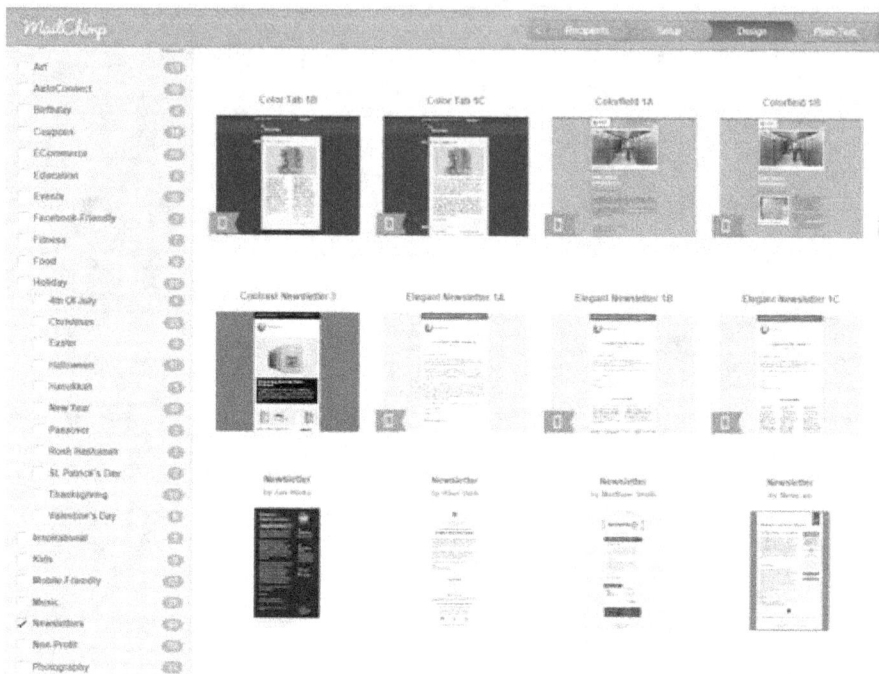

## Design

As you will notice, the options here are endless – we are thus going to cover a few of them that will be relevant and helpful to making your newsletter match your business branding. This is where you start to insert your content and change background and the font colors so that your newsletter remains unique to you.

Just click the boxes you would want to edit and begin to insert the news you collected. Simple!

The dashboard, which is similar to those in email programs that appear when you click in the box will contain all the tools you require to insert photos, change font size and color, use bullet points and so on.

**Our real estate agency is the best in the area...**

*Confirm and preview the newsletter*

When you're satisfied with the images and content, click confirm and go over what you've created using the preview button. If everything is okay, just follow the simple steps to finish the process.

*Click send*

Your newsletter will make your customers glad. If you used relevant and interesting content that shows your company is unique and a leader in the field to create your newsletter, your customers and prospective clients will remember you when they require your services.

Don't forget that in this program, the possibilities are endless so the next time you log in, be sure to check out what else you can do in the program and use it for your marketing program.

# Offline Strategies

We have a number of offline marketing strategies you can employ to make prospective real estate buyers and sellers to contact you. Also, unlike the online strategies, most of them are really straightforward and less taxing.

For instance, we have

### *Bandit signs*

Bandit signs are little variations of the usual billboard that are placed on walls or staked into the ground to act as the first point of contact for potential buyers (or sellers) and agents or marketers.

When drafting a design for your bandit signs, you have the option of visiting your local signs designer or look for a website that specializes in this field. When you're just starting out, make sure you order around 200 bandit signs while taking into account that a great number of them will be torn down or go missing.

## Billboard signs

To take your marketing efforts up a notch, you could rent a billboard and the easiest way is through an advertising agency. The costs vary a lot depending on the location and the agency itself. For a billboard measuring 14' by 48', for instance, you can expect to part with the following cash for a four-week rental:

$3,000- Atlanta, Georgia

$1,200-Albuquerque, New Mexico

$3,100- Indianapolis, Indiana

The location of the billboard is very important so make sure the billboard is located in an area, which many people pass through so that the billboard is effective. You should also consider the number of people that drive by every day and how much the drivers can actually see the billboard.

For more information about renting a billboard, visit https://www.lendvo.com/guide-renting-billboard/.

## Local media interviews

Getting a media interview can be difficult and that's why it's not the best idea to keep calling your local media house requesting for an interview. The best wat to get your name in front of the program directors and news directors is by writing and issuing relevant and pertinent press releases.

These need to be properly written and have to discuss critical issues of significance to their viewers. When you begin establishing yourself as an illustrious real estate expert, your phone will ring more often. These media appearances can really increase your exposure and advance your brand name recognition, which can bring about increased investment deals due to the perceived idea that you are an expert in the field. Many people that you'll be trying to sell properties to or those you will be trying to buy properties from will perhaps already know you. As such, they are likely to be more trusting thanks to your reputation within the local community.

### Seminars

You can also give free seminars in a niche that is related to real estate to grow the size of your portfolio. As a residential real estate agent, you could consider giving a free seminar about topics as extensive as "The best ways to sell your property for a price in a down market" to "Buying a home with terrible credit." The important thing here is not to market yourself directly but come across more like a financial planner. Show your prospective customers what you know, and how you can help them; they will be glad to show their money later on.

### Public speaking

Public speaking does not usually appear like a natural offline real estate marketing strategy, but it has potential that many people fail to consider. Most people are not natural public speakers; and do not quail if you are one of them. You can start by joining your local Toastmasters club and training with the best in the art of public speaking. Even as you are learning, you will be exposed to community and business leaders, many of whom have cash and (or) connections and could thus turn to be prime candidates to do business with.

### Inform everyone you know and in your networks

Every so often, fresh investors make their first deals with family and friends, and more so, the referrals they can offer. All the exceptional real estate marketing ideas in the world cannot make up for a formidable social network that can easily point you toward your first acquisition.

Nonetheless, the deals that fall into your laps cannot really materialize until people know you are in the business. Therefore, even before you make the leap, just tell them, and prepare them to work with you as you begin. Word of mouth is simple but also a great tool, which some people argue is one of the top most in real estate marketing.

So, just begin telling people what you are about because you never know from where that elusive first deal might arise.

Other strategies you could also use include the following:

- Magazines: Real estate magazines are a goldmine for real estate deals so make sure to use them

- MLS (Multiple listing service)

- Telemarketing: This is where you cold-call prospective customers to spread your company's message. You could call them yourself or use a call center to make large volume sales. You could use the calls as an opportunity to call your current clients to get feedback about their satisfaction, talk about new listings, contact houses that are listed as sale by owner etc.

- Direct mail: Just mail potential clients directly; make sure to package your marketing material in a captivating manner to ensure it stands out from the many mails that the customer might receive. In the mail, don't let it to scream 'buy my product'; make sure you have something useful in your mail e.g. an open house, the ideal time to move etc.

- Referrals from current clients: You could offer to incentivize them in a way. You could send gifts/cards to your clients during special occasions e.g. Christmas, birthday, thanksgiving, anniversary, housewarming etc. then remember to mention your referral program

- Network: Don't just rely on your social networks for leads; you could participate in chambers of commerce and various networking groups to meet prospective customers. Make sure that you are an active member of any organization that you join, as this will ensure you stand out from everybody else. Being active means attending seminars and various other meetings, being very active in organizing other seminars, sponsoring an event etc. Another creative way is to build mutually beneficial relationships with some of the participants in those groups whereby the other person offers something, just as you do. If you are into commercial real estate, you may want to attend broker meetings to help you generate good leads that could ultimately bring in some sales.

- Brochures

- Flyers

- Radio ads

- Television ads

- Newspapers targeting the specific target market

I strongly believe that the above information will help you to make significant progress in generating qualified leads that could easily convert to paying customers. The question you might be having now is; how do you close the deals? Let's discuss that.

# Step 4: Converting Leads into Closed Deals

By using the real estate marketing methods above, you will generate leads- but how do you convert these leads into real estate sales though?

Mainly, it's through follow-up and fulfillment.

**Follow-up**

According to statistics, about 48 percent of agents don't follow up with a prospect and 52 percent follow up at least once. Again, only 25 percent try contacting a prospect a second time and 12 percent try making three or more contacts.

You need to note that 80 percent of sales are made between the 5th to the 12th contact!

This essentially means that failing to retarget the lead is detrimental. When the lead mentions that they are not ready, you should not draw back but rather, keep contacting them and build a healthy relationship with the potential buyer; otherwise, he or she might get lost, feel ignored and perhaps fall into the hands of your competitor.

Therefore, you also need to get over the fear of offending your prospects by contacting them as many times as it takes because in real estate marketing, we say that by doing so, you are not badgering them, but being there when they are ready- because anyway, they are the ones who communicated that they are interested in the business.

**Fulfillment**

This simply refers to what you're giving them, the questions you are answering and the needs (of theirs) you are meeting.

Being there when they are ready is their most important need and it is accomplished through consistent follow-up. You also have to anticipate their questions and provide resources, answers and resolutions. While fulfillment is easier than follow-up it requires follow-up to accomplish. When you follow up, you meet their primary need.

## Nurture the lead

The agents who begin their relationship by offering informative and efficient customer service have a greater chance to build a stronger psychological and social bond with a prospect.

This bond can easily override your competitors and even if they don't buy at first, they will most likely have a sense of loyalty that will drive them back to you.

Tip: Develop the habit of reading-through your contacts and updating them to a special excel sheet so that you are up to date with all of them. After that, make sure you categorize them as hot, warm or cold. The hot leads should be the ones that are ready to buy while the warm or cold leads are still weighing their options. You should therefore be with them through the decision process placing effort accordingly, as per the category they belong to.

At this point, I believe you are ready to implement your plan, and then evaluate later on. Before that though;

## Do a quick analysis

Once you've known the basic elements of your real estate marketing strategy, you need to take a step back and review the details, making sure all you've planned is realistic.

Do you have considerable knowledge of your audience? Do you have the means to blog regularly (if you chose blogging as a strategy)? How about the timelines for success, are they practically possible? Comb over your plan before you begin to make sure you do not have to return to square one after months of work and reconfigure your marketing blueprint completely.

# Step 5: Implement Your Plan, Examine Your Tactics and Repeat

After setting your real estate marketing foundation, you can proceed to put everything into action. You can begin publishing landing pages, social media updates, blog posts, get your video and email strategies up and running or whatever else depending on what you selected as your marketing strategies, and begin implementing any other tactic you came across along the way you deem worthy of using.

After a period of about one month, take to Google Analytics and any other software you use to track and automate your marketing to go over the performance of your online marketing. Pin point what has worked so far, what has not and what you can do to advance your messaging, branding and eventually, bottom line.

In everything you do, realize that real estate marketing is like a machine that never stops- and this machine only grows stronger the more attention you pay to it and build upon it. You need to keep experimenting with fresh techniques you haven't tried yet and see whether they can assist you achieve your goals.

## Commit yourself to specific tasks

From the little tasks such as getting a responsive website to the bigger tactics like developing an email campaign, you need to break down the kind of real estate marketing activities you are committed to doing over a specified period of time. You don't have to worry about taking on everything on all at once; but it is important to identify the lighter daily tasks you can perform in minutes and other tasks that need more time, effort and perhaps money (the long term tasks). Let's take a look at that in more detail.

*The small short term tasks*

Think of the important items you can take care of within short durations of time. For instance, you can include the following tactics to implement in your spare time:

- Brainstorm some blog post ideas everyday

- Segment your list of contacts for your email campaign

- Optimize you real estate marketing website for search

- Create a social media posting program or schedule

- Do a research of the options in market automation software

- Work little by little on a piece of long-form content such as an e-book

The basis of your plan of real estate marketing is built on executing these tasks, so you need to find time to work on them. Tasks like developing blog post ideas for real estate is a continuous process, since blogging never ends, you need to split your time evenly on things that you'll need to take care of regularly and one time tasks that require to be complete immediately.

*The larger, long-term projects*

On the other side, we have bigger marketing efforts, which you'll realize are usually activities related to lead generation, earning commissions and closing deals. In any case, the whole idea of marketing is to bring more sales- so you need to remember the large-scale goals that are sustained by your daily and weekly marketing activities.

After one month of blogging for example, you can examine your Google analytics to observe how your posts are doing. Ask yourself- how long do users spend on each page or post? How many sessions or views have I received?

**Identify the metrics you'll build upon (in the online strategies)**

Every real estate agent has one metric they would want to improve- their commission; when it comes to marketing though, you need to determine all the areas you'd want to improve. For instance, you want people to better know about your brand; thus, improving your web traffic could be a good goal to start with. If you're looking to ramp up lead generation, then having your site optimized with lead capture forms and capabilities should be your primary goal here. Perhaps you want to cultivate future sellers; this means that improving the email list could be your best bet. Just plan your real estate ideas around the metrics, whichever they are.

Perhaps (just like most beginners) you are not really sure about what could be the most important metrics for your marketing; you can check this graph from a report of content marketing institute and marketing profs. It shows what many professionals and brands out there consider the most essential metrics for their marketing. You have to note that getting site visitors is looked at as very crucial when it comes to success in online marketing- in any case, it's a substantial sales driver.

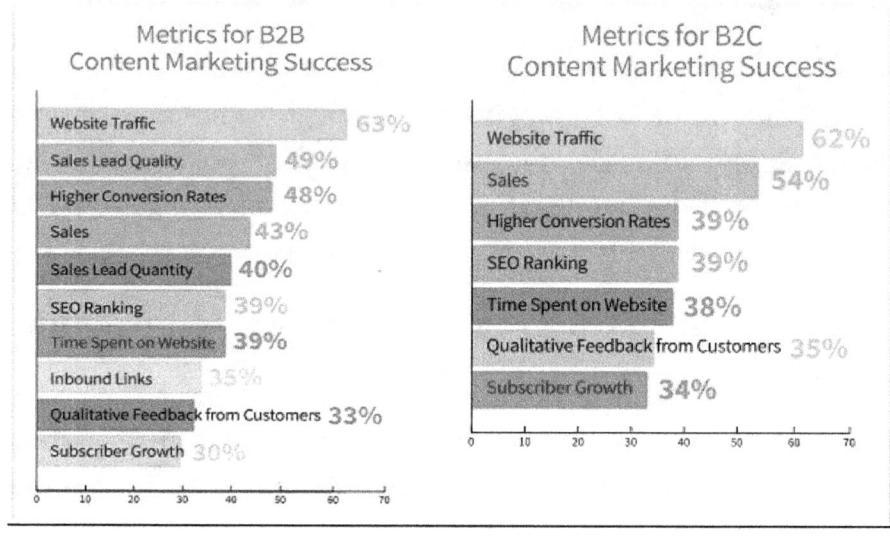

# Conclusion

We have come to the end of the book. Thank you for reading and congratulations for reading until the end.

Many people usually have the dream of being successful with real estate marketing, but few of them know how to go about it. They don't know where to start, what to start with and how.

In this regard, the book has given you a plan that you can follow.

Use it as a blueprint- add whichever strategies you want to the ones already discussed and implement them when you're ready. Don't forget to do a proper analysis of the plan before implementation though and when you're done, evaluate everything, making sure to focus on areas that you could improve.

If you found the book valuable, can you recommend it to others? One way to do that is to post a review on Amazon.

Click here to leave a review for this book on Amazon!

Thank you and good luck!

www.ingramcontent.com/pod-product-compliance
Lightning Source LLC
Chambersburg PA
CBHW071237220526
45468CB00002B/893